THE GROUP OF SEVEN
COLOURING BOOK

The Group of Seven brought together Canadian artists who were searching for a new way to paint. They wanted to make art that helped people understand the way our Canadian landscape looked and felt. Their names were Franklin Carmichael, Lawren S. Harris, A.Y. Jackson, F.H. Varley, Arthur Lismer, J.E.H. MacDonald and Frank Johnston, who left the group and was later replaced by A.J. Casson. Tom Thomson is often considered an honorary member of the Group of Seven. He joined them on many painting trips, but drowned in Algonquin Park before the group formed.

In this colouring book, you will find 22 paintings of lakes, forests and mountains by Thomson and the Group of Seven. They are shown as small pictures on the inside front and back covers. You will notice that the painters did not try to make a painting that looked like a photograph. Instead, they used bold brush strokes and simple shapes to tell the story of what it felt like to be in that place. When you colour in these pictures, you can either try to copy the original colours and style, or you might decide to use your own.

The last page of this book is blank so that you can draw and colour in your own picture. Find a hill, a group of trees or a row of houses, and see if you can capture them on the page.

Pomegranate

1. Tom Thomson (1877–1917), *The West Wind,* 1916–1917. Oil on canvas, 120.7 x 137.9 cm (47½ x 54⁵⁄₁₆ in.). Art Gallery of Ontario, Toronto. Gift of the Canadian Club of Toronto, 1926. © 2009 Art Gallery of Ontario

2. Franklin Carmichael (1890–1945), *Jackfish Village,* 1926. Watercolour and graphite on paper, 50.8 x 56.7 cm (20 x 22⁵⁄₁₆ in.). Art Gallery of Ontario, Toronto. Gift of the Canadian National Exhibition Association, 1965. © 2009 Estate of Franklin Carmichael / Art Gallery of Ontario

3. Tom Thomson (1877–1917), *Marguerites, Wood Lilies and Vetch,* 1915. Oil on wood, 21.4 x 26.8 cm (8⁷⁄₁₆ x 10⁹⁄₁₆ in.). Art Gallery of Ontario, Toronto. Gift from the Albert H. Robson Memorial Subscription Fund, 1941. © 2009 Art Gallery of Ontario

4. Lawren S. Harris (1885–1970), *Spruce and Snow, Northern Ontario,* 1916. Oil on canvas, 102.3 x 115.3 cm (40¼ x 45⅜ in.). Art Gallery of Ontario, Toronto. Gift of Roy G. Cole, Rosseau, Ontario, 1991. © 2009 Estate of Lawren S. Harris

5. J.E.H. MacDonald (1873–1932), *Mount Goodsir, Yoho Park,* 1925. Oil on canvas, 107.3 x 122.3 cm (42¼ x 48⅛ in.). Art Gallery of Ontario, Toronto. Gift of Dr. and Mrs. Max Stern, Dominion Gallery, Montreal, 1979. © 2009 Art Gallery of Ontario

6. Franklin Carmichael (1890–1945), *Mattawa,* 1935. Graphite, watercolour and gouache on paper, 55.7 x 43.5 cm (21¹⁵⁄₁₆ x 17⅛ in.). Art Gallery of Ontario, Toronto. Gift of John R. Casey, Q.C., Toronto, 1996. © 2009 Estate of Franklin Carmichael / Art Gallery of Ontario

7. Lawren S. Harris (1885–1970), *Lake, Algonquin Park,* n.d. Oil on board, 30.5 x 38.1 cm (11¹⁵⁄₁₆ x 15 in.). Art Gallery of Ontario, Toronto. Gift from the Friends of Canadian Art Fund, 1938. © 2009 Estate of Lawren S. Harris

8. A.J. Casson (1898–1992), *Old Store at Salem,* 1931. Oil on canvas, 76.7 x 91.5 cm (30³⁄₁₆ x 36 in.). Art Gallery of Ontario, Toronto. Gift from the J.S. McLean Collection, by Canada Packers Inc., Toronto, 1990. © 2009 Art Gallery of Ontario

9. Lawren S. Harris (1885–1970), *Lake and Mountains,* 1928. Oil on canvas, 130.8 x 160.6 cm (51½ x 63¼ in.). Art Gallery of Ontario, Toronto. Gift from the Fund of the T. Eaton Co. Ltd. for Canadian Works of Art, 1948. © 2009 Estate of Lawren S. Harris

10. Tom Thomson (1877–1917), *The Canoe,* spring or fall 1914. Oil on canvas, 17.3 x 25.3 cm (6¹³⁄₁₆ x 9¹⁵⁄₁₆ in.). Art Gallery of Ontario, Toronto. Gift from the J.S. McLean Collection, Toronto, 1969; donated by the Ontario Heritage Foundation, 1988. © 2009 Art Gallery of Ontario

11. Franklin Carmichael (1890–1945), *La Cloche Mountain and Lake,* c. 1940. Oil on plywood panel, 29.9 x 40.4 cm (11¾ x 15⅞ in.). Art Gallery of Ontario, Toronto. Gift from the J.S. McLean Collection, Toronto, by Canada Packers Inc., 1990. © 2009 Estate of Franklin Carmichael / Art Gallery of Ontario

12. Lawren S. Harris (1885–1970), *Algoma Lake,* c. 1920. Oil on panel, 26.7 x 35.6 cm (10½ x 14 in.). Art Gallery of Ontario, Toronto. Gift from the Friends of Canadian Art Fund, 1938. © 2009 Estate of Lawren S. Harris

13. Arthur Lismer (1885–1969), *Sunlight in a Wood,* 1930. Oil on canvas, 91.4 x 101.6 cm (36 x 40 in.). Art Gallery of Ontario, Toronto. Bequest of John M. Lyle, Toronto, 1946. © 2009 Estate of Arthur Lismer

14. Lawren S. Harris (1885–1970), *Grey Day, Lake Superior,* c. 1922. Oil on pulpboard, 30.3 x 38.1 cm (11¹⁵⁄₁₆ x 15 in.). Art Gallery of Ontario, Toronto. Gift from the Friends of Canadian Art Fund, 1938. © 2009 Estate of Lawren S. Harris

15. A.Y. Jackson (1882–1974), *Near Murray Bay, Quebec,* n.d. Oil on panel, 21.4 x 26.7 cm (8⁷⁄₁₆ x 10½ in.). Art Gallery of Ontario, Toronto. Gift of Mrs. Doris Huestis Mills Speirs, Pickering, Ontario, 1971. © Courtesy of the Estate of the late Dr. Naomi Jackson Groves

16. Franz (Frank) Johnston (1888–1949), *Cowboy Camp, Sundown, Lake Louise, Alberta,* 1925. Oil on board, 23.3 x 33.6 cm (9³⁄₁₆ x 13¼ in.). Art Gallery of Ontario, Toronto. Purchase, with the assistance of R.W. Finlayson, Toronto, 1970. © 2009 Art Gallery of Ontario

17. Arthur Lismer (1885–1969), *Lily Pond, Georgian Bay,* 1948. Oil on canvas board, 40.5 x 50.5 cm (15¹⁵⁄₁₆ x 19⅞ in.). Art Gallery of Ontario, Toronto. Gift of the Estate of Roy Fraser Elliott, 2005. © 2009 Estate of Arthur Lismer

18. J.E.H. MacDonald (1873–1932), *The Elements,* 1916. Oil on board, 71.1 x 91.8 cm (28 x 36⅛ in.). Art Gallery of Ontario, Toronto. Gift of Dr. Lorne Pierce, Toronto, 1958, in memory of Edith Chown Pierce (1890–1954). © 2009 Art Gallery of Ontario

19. Franklin Carmichael (1890–1945), *Autumn Hillside,* 1920. Oil on canvas, 76.2 x 91.4 cm (30 x 36 in.). Art Gallery of Ontario, Toronto. Gift from the J.S. McLean Collection, Toronto, 1969; donated by the Ontario Heritage Foundation, 1988. © 2009 Art Gallery of Ontario

20. J.E.H. MacDonald (1873–1932), *Falls, Montreal River,* 1920. Oil on canvas, 121.9 x 153 cm (48 x 60¼ in.). Art Gallery of Ontario, Toronto. Purchase, 1933. © 2009 Art Gallery of Ontario

21. Tom Thomson (1877–1917), *Autumn Foliage,* fall or winter 1915. Oil on wood, 21.6 x 26.8 cm (8½ x 10½ in.). Art Gallery of Ontario, Toronto. Gift from the Reuben and Kate Leonard Canadian Fund, 1927. © 2009 Art Gallery of Ontario

22. A.J. Casson (1898–1992), *Jack Pine and Poplar,* 1948. Oil on tempered hardboard, 76.2 x 91.4 cm (30 x 36 in.). Art Gallery of Ontario, Toronto. Gift of Salada-Shirriff-Horsey Limited, 1959. © 2009 Art Gallery of Ontario

Pomegranate Communications, Inc.
19018 NE Portal Way, Portland OR 97230
800 227 1428
www.pomegranate.com

Pomegranate Europe Ltd.
Unit 1, Heathcote Business Centre, Hurlbutt Road
Warwick, Warwickshire CV34 6TD, UK
[+44] 0 1926 430111
sales@pomeurope.co.uk

© 2009 Art Gallery of Ontario, Toronto

Catalog No. CB108

Designed by Gina Bostian

Printed in Korea

24 23 22 21 20 19   12 11 10 9 8 7 6 5 4

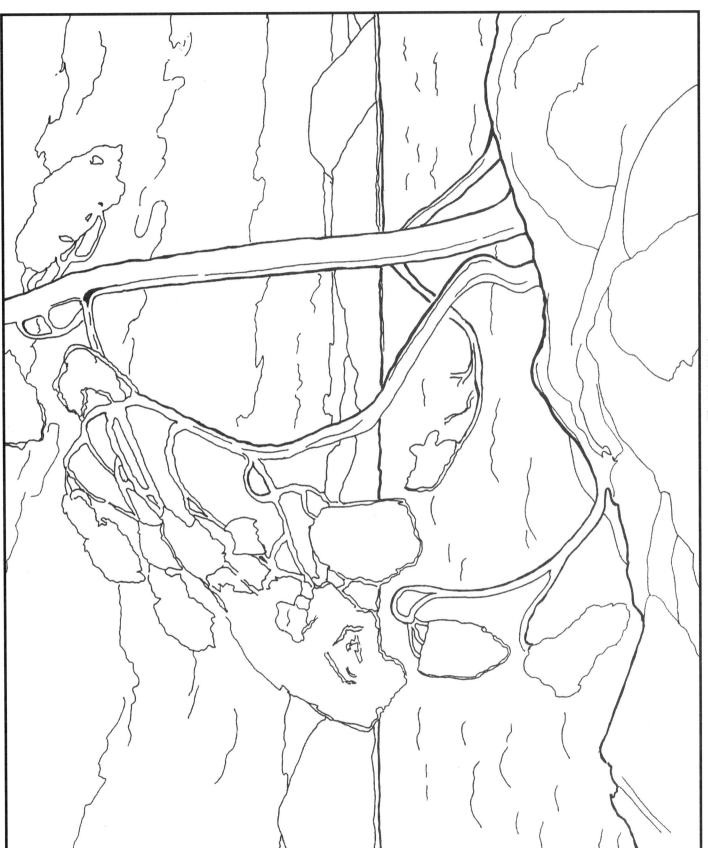

1. Tom Thomson, *The West Wind*

2. Franklin Carmichael, *Jackfish Village*

3. Tom Thomson, *Marguerites, Wood Lilies and Vetch*

4. Lawren S. Harris, *Spruce and Snow, Northern Ontario*

5. J.E.H. MacDonald, *Mount Goodsir, Yoho Park*

6. Franklin Carmichael, *Mattawa*

7. Lawren S. Harris, *Lake, Algonquin Park*

8. A.J. Casson, *Old Store at Salem*

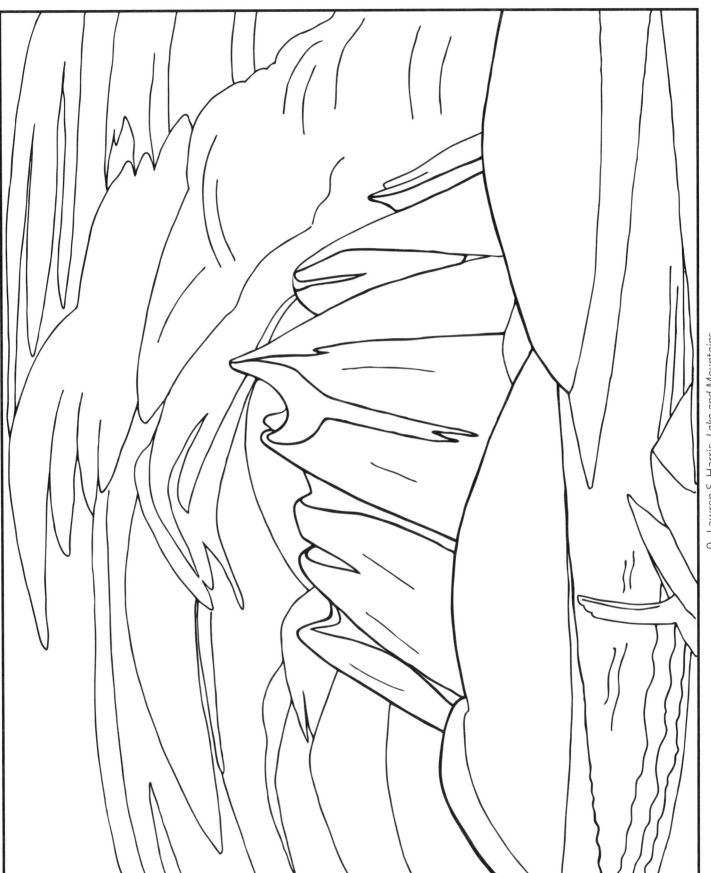

9. Lawren S. Harris, *Lake and Mountains*

10. Tom Thomson, *The Canoe*

11. Franklin Carmichael, *La Cloche Mountain and Lake*

12. Lawren S. Harris, *Algoma Lake*

13. Arthur Lismer, *Sunlight in a Wood*

14. Lawren S. Harris, *Grey Day, Lake Superior*

15. A.Y. Jackson, *Near Murray Bay, Quebec*

16. Franz (Frank) Johnston, *Cowboy Camp, Sundown, Lake Louise, Alberta*

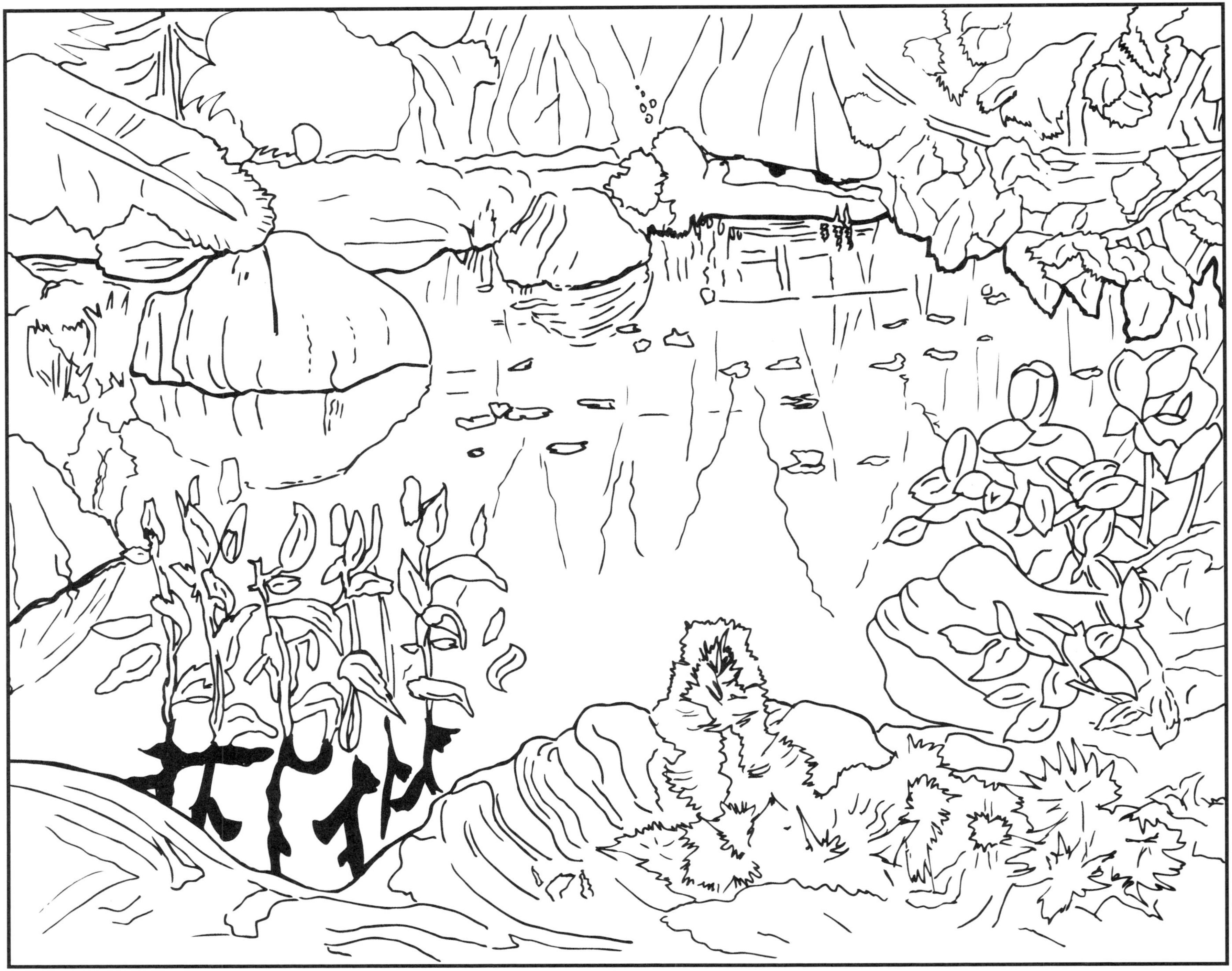

17. Arthur Lismer, *Lily Pond, Georgian Bay*

18. J.E.H. MacDonald, *The Elements*

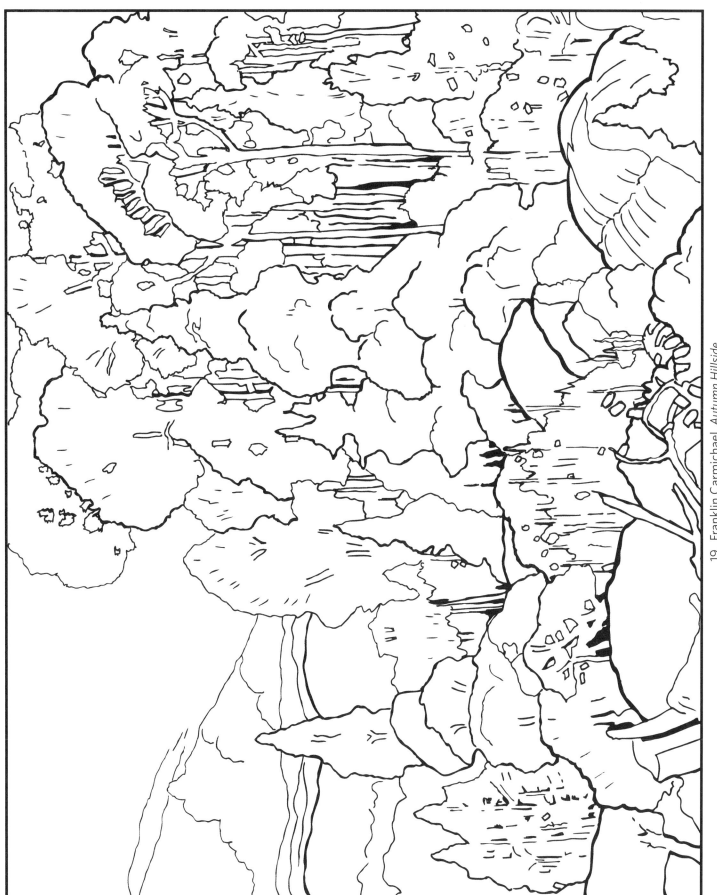

19. Franklin Carmichael, *Autumn Hillside*

20. J.E.H. MacDonald, *Falls, Montreal River*

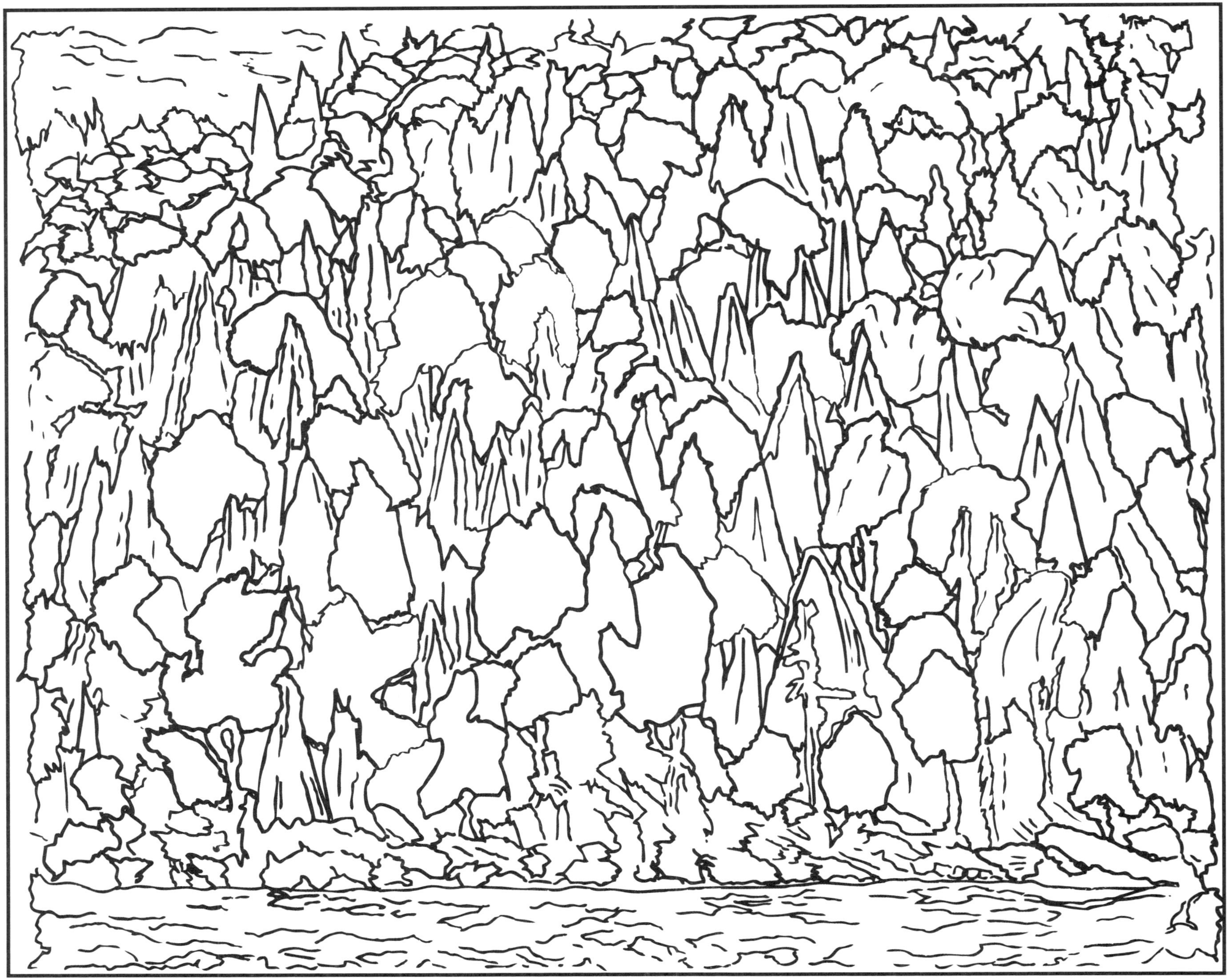

21. Tom Thomson, *Autumn Foliage*

22. A.J. Casson, *Jack Pine and Poplar*

Draw and colour your own picture here!